A Mother Twice Over

Jewel Pastor

BookLeaf Publishing

Presentation by *BookLeaf Publishing*

Web: www.bookleafpub.com

E-mail: info@bookleafpub.com

ISBN: 9789357616591

First edition 2022

*To my husband, Ruel, and my children,
Hana and Sean, without whom this book
would have not been written*

If You Want Me To

If you want a cuddle, I will give you one.
If you want milk, you can have all that you
want.
If you want me close, I will stay by your side.
If you want to sleep on my tummy, I will give
you that ride.

I know there will come a day
That I will put you down
And you will not want to be picked up anymore,
A day when tight hugs and butterfly kisses will
be too much
And you will want cuddles no more.

So while I still can,
I will cuddle you, kiss you, hold your hand.
I will feel your tiny heart beat while you sleep
on my tummy.
I will love you the way only a mother like me
can.

Please Remember...

Watching you sleep on my lap,
I wonder how long you'll stay as tiny—
Tiny hands, tiny feet, tiny nose, tiny lips.
My heart swells with happiness
As I looked at you intently
For you are my dream fulfilled.
I hope when you are all grown up and
No longer need your Mummy,
You'll find a way to remember—
Remember that you once slept on my lap
While everything about you was tiny
And my heart has always been yours.

Loving You

A feeling rests in my heart.
It sings the same melody
just as the first day,
only the song is
sweeter and louder.
I am used to the feeling.
But today is different.
Today, I smile 'cause of the life
who is the source
of the feeling, of the song.
I love you, my daughter.

A Poem for You

I caught myself again
staring at you—
You who contentedly sleep
with one of your cheeks
resting on my chest.

I love the way it feels
looking at you—
You who blissfully dream
with one of your arms
reaching for the sky.

I did not expect
feeling so much for you—
You who were wonderfully made
by the almighty Creator
turning me into a mother.

I surprise even myself
being able to care for you—
You who changed my life
by your mere presence
inspiring me to be better.

But I'm Still Here

The morning light has already
Seeped through the curtains
But you're still sound asleep.
I listen to your gentle breathing.
I feel the warmth of your tiny body
As you snuggled so close to me.
I smell the fragrance of your hair.
I taste the salt in my tears
As I realised we are bound to part again.
I see you open your eyes
And flash that sweet grin at me.
The morning light has already
Seeped through the curtains
But I'm still here.

Birth Day No.2

Woke up early.
Took a shower.
Ate a little.
Waited a lot.
Felt those contractions.
Hurt very much.
Twisted my back.
Asked for relief.
Took a nap.
(Big sister) took a peak.
(Daddy) took a video.
(Baby) finally came out.
Watched siblings meet.
Melted my heart.
Took a photo.
Took a shower.
Handed (baby) to nurse.
Slept at last.

I Love You, My Son

I love you, my son.
You're my prayer answered
And my dream come true.

I love you, my son.
You're proof that God listens
And he definitely loves me.

I love you, my son.
You bring joy to my heart
And make me feel complete.

I love you, my son.
You drive me crazy at times
And make me question things.

Nevertheless…

I love you, my son.
You challenge me in many ways
And you inspire me to be better every day.

Nobody Knows

Nobody knows I wish I were a much better
mother every day.
I wish I were so much more patient
That I never get cross, never yell, and never
frown.
I wish I have unlimited compassion and
unbridled kindness
That I never ever hurt you and make you cry.
I wish I have all the time in the world
That I can listen to one more story or play one
more game.
I wish I get to live forever
That I can undo all wrongs and make sure only
the good are remembered.
Nobody knows I wish my love and what I do
with what I know
Will always be enough for you…

Another Late Night
(Another Early Morning)

Another late night.
Restlessness.
Another story,
Another drink,
Another bite,
Another rolling of
The toy train
On its tracks.

Another early morning.
Exhaustion.
Just woken up.
That barking dog.
At 5:45 am.
Thank you though.
Slept through the night
And woke up with you two
By my side.

Seasons of a Mother's Life

Spring it seems to me were
The days my babies were born
The long stretches of sleepless nights
The nursing that goes on for years
Their first teeth, first steps, first words
My children's first attempts at learning

Summer it seems to me will be
The nine to threes spent away from me
The school runs and playdates
The everyday homework and projects
The changing moods and temperament
My children's many years at school

Fall it seems to me will be
The empty nester's stage
The desire to explore and find oneself
The wish to be seen and loved
The urge to move out and settle down
My children's twenties and thirties perhaps

Winter it seems to me will be
The twilight years for my husband and I
The arrival of sweet grandchildren
The years when my kids will find their way back
The many days when I'd reflect whether I've
done enough
My children's turn to think about the seasons of
life

Muddy Puddle

12

Splash! went little feet,
Shrieks of joy—little pool spits,
Wet socks, happy hearts…

Remember When

Remember when you were by yourself?
You were my only child.
You were always with me.
'What happened, Mum?' you asked.

Remember when I told you I have a baby in my
tummy?
You were so ecstatic.
You wanted a baby sister.
'Can I call her Peachy Nina please?' you
pleaded.

Remember when we found out that you were
going to have a brother?
You were not too happy.
You even shed a few tears.
'Why did he have to be a boy?' you buzzed.

Remember when your brother was born?
You took a peak while he was coming out.
You let out a scream of excitement.
'Can I give him a hug?!' you begged.

Remember when I couldn't spend as much time with you as before?
You were confused at first.
You adjusted nevertheless.
'Why are you crying, Mum?' you wanted to know.

Remember when I told you that you were the best?
You smiled at me with that gorgeous smile of yours.
Your beaming face told me you loved it.
'Why are you so wonderful, my daughter?' I wanted to know.

My Mum Life

Getting up at the crack of dawn
Saying a prayer for myself and the family
Cooking everyone's breakfast
Packing everybody's lunch
Kissing you all goodbye
Rushing to work one more time
Teaching the whole day
Thinking about all of you
Rushing to get back home
Coming home to hugs and laughter
Mothering till it's time to go to bed
Feeling the love in my heart
Thanking the Lord for another day
And the chance to do it all over again…

A Mother's Heart

It's like a time machine,
Travelling from one milestone to another at a
whim
and remembering how important they were.

Or like a sponge,
Absorbing every loving word said to each other
and soaking in every tender moment
experienced.

Or like a treasure chest,
Storing memories of fun times together
and keeping safe every smile and laughter
shared.

Or like a woman's purse,
Carrying an indomitable spirit
and an unquenchable thirst to see my children
succeed in life.

My pride, my love, my memories, my power…
All in a mother's heart.

My Daughter

Ah, who is this lass with twinkling eyes
With soft voice and laughter so nice
Who tosses back her long, black hair
Skips around the house, giving no care

She asks a million questions of late
While dishing out facts like she's 28
She does a pirouette and makes a bow
Draws pictures adroitly—I don't know how

She reaches for my face and gives me a kiss
Moments like this I hope I'll never miss
Her gentle nature and very kind heart
I hope she never loses when her teen years start

Fondness

A giant ball of cuteness on two chubby legs
The refreshing scent of soap, milk, and fresh
bread
The soothing and calm colour of powder blue
Baby soft, smooth skin and squishy pink cheeks
Singing songs before we go to sleep
The taste of each heartfelt smooch
The sweet, sweet sound of someone calling me
Mum

Mother's Day

It's Mother's Day every day when I'm with you
Your hugs and kisses always see me through
A gentle wipe of my falling tears
A kind and loving word right in my ears
A soothing touch when we hold hands
Our exciting trips to very strange lands
I don't need chocolates or flowers
All I need are memories and hours
Of tender love and togetherness
These are enough to bring me happiness

When You Grow Up

When you
Grow up, children,
Will you remember me
Saying to you how much I love
You so?

Will you
Remember me
Carrying you inside
Me, in my heart, and in my arms?
Will you?

Will you
Know that I think
About you every second,
Every minute of every day?
Will you?

Will you
Be able to
Tell that I cared for you
No matter what and for all time?
Will you?

When you
Grow up, will you
Remember all these and
More, my dearest children, my loves?
Hope so.